# *Thoughts* From the

# Bench

## *of* Life

*Anecdotes & Observations*
*From a Small-Town Journalist*

## Debbie Meehan

**Colonia Corner**
**Colonia, NJ**

Thoughts From the Bench of Life
Anecdotes & Observations From a Small-Town Journalist
Copyright © 2023 Debbie Meehan

ISBN: 979-8-9888522-0-9

Published by
Colonia Corner
Colonia, NJ


Printed in the United States of America

Cover Design by Eric Labacz
www.labaczdesign.com

*This book is dedicated to my three children,*
*Kayla, Sean Patrick and Timothy.*
*You will always be my reasons*
*for every season of my life.*

# Contents

# Introduction
## *The Lake House*

And so this is where my story begins.

Sometimes the best way to cleanse your soul and remember who you used to be is to take in a deep breath of fresh air. Not the air you normally breathe, but rather air that is new, that is clean, that is silent. As the winds of life blow, millions of little fragments find their way to cling onto us. Sometimes you have to shake off the dust, keep the pieces that shine then let the wind blow the rest away.

I recently decided that I needed a couple of days of sabbatical from my everyday life. I packed a bag and rented a small cabin on the lake. Alone on this adventure, it was just me and my computer. This was quite a bold move for me as I normally do not like being alone. I would much rather be surrounded by friends and family. Unfortunately, I was feeling burnt out, a little lost, and I needed to reconnect with the person I used to be. I decided I wanted to finally start writing that book I always promised myself I would write. The project I kept putting aside for another day. It was during that peaceful time away on the lake that I began to put together this book.

As I sat outside my rustic little cabin overlooking the tranquil water, five ducks and two swans floated in perfect harmony in front of me. Seriously, I couldn't have made up a more perfect backdrop if I tried. Hoping to gain some clarity and purpose, I could now do so with hope in my heart. I wasn't quite sure what inspiration I would find during my time at the lake or even what I would write about. What I did want to discover was the part of myself I had lost. Getting that part of me back would give me the strength to figure the rest of it out. I'm referring to the person I was before the world got so hard. The person who was carefree and had more empathy for people. I felt as though those parts of me were slipping away, and I refused to let that part of me go because they were the parts I liked best about myself.

So amid a brief quiet in the storm of everyday life, I started to find the old me and began this journey to write my book. Honestly, it wasn't terribly difficult. It was just a matter of peeling off the layers that were weighing me down, exhausting me and challenging the person I was meant to be. While watching the storm blow back out across the water, so too did the layers that I no longer wanted upon me.

Sometimes in life we all need to take a deep breath, shake off the fragments of life that are weighing us down and refocus our lens until we see the world in a better light.

It may not always be easy during these trying times, but the world really is a beautiful place. Unlike the five ducks and the two swans who swam in perfect harmony on that tranquil lake, we will never all float around in perfect harmony with the masses of the world. But we can find our own lake and our own swan and our own little cabin to run away to every now and then when the world gets to be too much. Sometimes we all just need to hit the refresh button, straighten our crowns and start again.

That's when the healing begins and life continues.

# Chapter 1
## *From the Bench of Life*

It's a scene that plays out on any ballfield, in any town, in any state. I was standing along the fence as the ball players came off the field after a big game. The first group of players that came were all smiles, hugging each other as their team clinched the game that would advance them to the championships. The second set of players exited the field a little sad, but they immediately headed to the snack stand to ease their disappointment with a big dish of ice cream or a sweet treat. Although one team was happy and the other team discouraged, at the end of the day the players would remain friends and return to their normal routine. After all, these baseball players were only nine years old. It was just a game.

Unfortunately, one young player would remember this day much longer than his teammates. As he walked off the field crying, his father, who was standing right behind him, began yelling at him. Instead of comforting the young player, he told him he should feel bad, he was a terrible player and that it was his fault the team lost. This is just the part I heard, and it was more than I needed to hear. His father continued to belittle him as the young boy bravely walked past his teammates, looking in the other direction so as to not show his tears. His father did not care who heard him.

This parent acted as if a group of nine-year-olds losing a baseball game was the end of the world. Not only was his behavior inexcusable, he broke his child's heart. I watched with tears in my eyes as this father and son drove away. I wanted to take this dad in my car and take him back in time. Perhaps a time before so much anger was pent up inside him that he had to lash out and humiliate his young son at a baseball game. I wanted to share some touching stories that I have witnessed with the hope of him realizing what's really important in life.

The first place I would take this parent would be to a skating party for a little girl named Bethany. This young child had been trying to celebrate her birthday for three years but, unfortunately, was too sick from her chemo treatments. Bethany was diagnosed with leukemia two weeks after her sixth birthday. This child who had been fighting for her life was finally able to celebrate her ninth birthday with family and friends. She may have fallen once or twice because she didn't really know how to skate but no one yelled at her for not being the best skater. They simply picked her up and thanked God that she was able to fall while learning to skate. Watching the results of a baseball game and watching your child fight for their life cannot even be compared.

Fast-forward a few weeks to a baseball benefit for Eric LeGrand. Eric was a defensive tackle for Rutgers University when, at the age of twenty-one, he became paralyzed from the neck down after colliding with another player. Eric was wheeled onto the baseball field with his cousin and mom to throw out the first pitch. The entire stadium stood up and applauded this young athlete whose courage and motivation has inspired millions of people. My son and I had the privilege to escort Eric and his family up to a suite where he could watch the game comfortably. As we settled Eric in, I noticed that his family acted no different than other families. Eric and his mom argued over how many mozzarella sticks he was allowed to eat. As his mom and I spoke, I watched Eric out of the corner of my eye making silly faces at his cousin and laughing. The smile and joy in his eyes never left his face, not even for a minute. Throughout the day I sent up a few visitors to his suite. Each person came back down to the game with a smile on their face after spending time with Eric. Here's a young man who will never walk again but also a young man who never loses his positivity and ability to teach people what matters most in life. During a quiet moment alone when I stood next to Eric facing the baseball field, he told me that he missed playing football. Looking onto the baseball field from his wheelchair that afternoon, I think the last thing that would have crossed his mind, if he were able to play football, baseball or any other sport again, was not whether his team won or lost. I'm sure his only wish would be that he could play the game just one more time.

The final destination before I bring this father back to the baseball field and the son that he just humiliated would be the most difficult one of all. I would have him stand alongside a grieving family who just lost their eleven-year-old son to cancer. I would let him see the tears and the incomprehensible grief caused by the loss of their precious young child. I would want him to witness how this boy's death affected not only his family but an entire community that cared about him. It certainly did not matter what this little boy excelled at, or his failures. What mattered was that he was truly loved and that somehow his family would have to try and make sense of the unimaginable and find a way to heal. I am sure this family would do anything in the world to turn back the hands of time and have one more day with him. Unfortunately, they can only hold onto his memory.

At the end of this journey in time I would return this angry father back to the baseball field where I had witnessed what had happened. I would rewind time for just a few moments and place him back moments before the game ended. Would he still walk off with angry words strong enough to make his child hang his head in shame? Or would what he had seen through our journey soften his heart and remind him how very fragile life can be?

If your child is healthy and strong enough to sing a song, ride a bike or play baseball, count your blessings. Whether he or she wins or loses, misses the ball or gets a home run, if you are lucky enough to watch your child from the bench of life you truly are blessed. Sometimes it takes looking through the eyes of someone less fortunate to remind us what truly matters. Too many times we get caught up in being the best, comparing ourselves to others and possessing the finest things that life slips by us, and we forget to embrace the simplicity. Life hands us many things that we are unable to change, such as children who are sick, the death of a parent or other life events. We can, however, change things we cause ourselves, a word spoken in anger or a word not spoken at all. We have the power to change all the negativity if we choose to do so.

Tomorrow morning when you wake up and are able to get out of bed, raise the blinds and be grateful for the sunshine. If your biggest worry of the day is how you are going to get through all the laundry, plan that big party or take your son to his baseball game, consider yourself blessed.

What a gift to live life.

# Chapter 2
## *The Brown Station Wagon*

Let's face it: We would all like to have more than we do. We pass by a beautiful home and think to ourselves how nice it would be to live there. We see a fancy car and think how nice it would be to drive one. We clean out our closet, glancing out the window at the neighbors' new big addition, and think how much better life would be with just a little more room.

In my childhood days, the home I grew up in looked like everyone else's on the block. Most moms stayed home because one income was enough. I shared a room with my two sisters (and p.s. we did not have our own private bathroom), children played outside with each other until the streetlights came on and then together, as a family, we sat down to eat dinner every single night.

When my parents were starting out, they didn't have much but it never stopped them from packing up my three siblings and I into the old brown station wagon filled with camping equipment and heading to the mountains. It was a simple vacation, one my parents could afford, and we loved it because that's all we knew. As I think of my dad today it brings me back to the memory of his old brown station wagon.

You know the one. It had brown panels on the sides, and with the seats laid down it could fit just about every kid in the neighborhood. I never thought much about that car because that's what everyone in my neighborhood drove. It wasn't fancy, but in that time no one really had fancy cars; if they did, I don't remember them. What does come to mind is where that old brown station wagon took us as children.

No, it didn't take us to the airport for a trip to the islands. Instead, it took us up to the mountains where we would camp as a family, sit by fires and rock-hop in the streams that ran past the campsite. Sometimes we would get lost in the woods for hours exploring the beauty of Mother Nature. There was a trail we would follow up the mountain that would take us to a spot called Look Out Point, and through a child's eyes it seemed you could see the entire world from there. Then we'd walk back down and run through the cornfields, pick wild berries and stop to lie down in the open field so that we could look up at the sky and find pictures in the clouds. My dad told us if we stared long enough into the clouds, we could picture just about anything, and we did.

Then, as that old brown station wagon made its way down the mountain, instead of watching TV and playing video games in the car, my dad would make a game out of counting cows or license plates while reminiscing about the weekend we had just spent together. Sometimes my dad would even pull that station wagon to the side of the road and pick wildflowers for us. As kids, the times we spent together in that brown station wagon, coming home from the places it took us, were where our finest childhood memories were made.

My dad taught us not to worry about the little things because they are far less troubling than the burdens of life so many others must carry. He taught us to be kind to others always, to smile, to help people who needed a hand without judgement and just love. Follow those simple rules, he would say, and you will live a rich life.

It makes me wonder if that fancy car in the driveway of the billion-dollar home ever took the time to see the beauty of the mountains or feel the tranquility and peace that comes along while watching the sun set over the ocean like that good old brown station wagon did. Those are the gifts that life gives us at no extra cost, and those gifts are ones that can never put you into debt. Sometimes the things in life that give you the most happiness are the things that you pass by as you rush out the door to find something better.

My dad has since passed but the values and love he instilled in us have not. I still think about the brown station wagon from time to time, and it makes me smile as I count my blessings, knowing that we were so rich in life to have it.

# Chapter 3
## *The Human Race*

We all see the world through different eyes. Sometimes we feel positive, hopeful and loved. Yet, other times we feel negative, uncertain and weary.

Only we can decide how we choose to look at the world and how we chose in our own hearts to live these days we've been given.

It was a Friday night in January of 2022. I spent the evening with one of my best friends in the world. We don't always get to see each other as much as we would like but when we do it's as if time has never passed. We decided instead of going out she would come to my house and I would make dinner; after all, we didn't need to go to a crowded bar or restaurant because we just wanted to catch up, something time doesn't always allow us to do. My house was empty that evening, and I was excited to spend time with my friend as I happily prepared dinner. As I did so, the evening news came on. I knew what the top story; I, along with the rest of the world was watching all week. It was the tragic story of the death of a young black man named Tyre Nichols. The reporter spoke of how that evening at seven p.m. a video would be released to show the world what had happened to him at the hands of police officers. Instead of watching, I turned the TV off and put on some music as my girlfriend came through the door. Judge me as you will, but I just wasn't ready or prepared to watch that video, not just yet.

My friend and I had the best night. We cooked, had a beautiful bottle of Caymus wine (if you drink wine you know how great that bottle is), played a game, talked about our families, laughed and enjoyed our cherished friendship that was created through our children twenty-six years ago. It was a much-needed evening away from the rest of the world.

The next morning I put on a pot of coffee and was about to turn on the morning news, which I always do, but instead chose to do things around the house. A few hours later while straightening up the living room I looked at the TV and finally sat down and turned it on. I was ready, or so I thought.

I was horrified at what I saw. I watched for a while in tears and then had to turn it off because I felt so sad that this world was once again on fire. I felt heartbroken for that young man who lost his life and all those who loved him, especially his mom.

I just sat there for a while, trying to wrap my head around it all, as I did my son came down the stairs. He asked me if I was ok. I told him I was, and then he said he would see me later as he left for work.

When I heard him shut the door behind him, for the first time I felt terrified. I've been scared before as a mom, and if you're a parent you have been, too. Whether it was their first day of school or they had a fever, drove away with their new license, left for college or any reason, big or small, that took them away from your protected arms, they were all real reasons to worry. But this day, after watching the news, something inside of me left me feeling terrified.

For I am the mother of a son who just became a police officer. I prayed as he left for work that day, dressed proudly in his uniform, that he, whom I raised to be kind and compassionate, would not be harmed because of what he chose to do with his life, and that is to serve and protect his community. I also prayed for peace in this world and that no one, not one human being, would be harmed in light of this tragedy.

Bad things happen in this world, horrible tragic things, but there is also goodness and human kindness, and sometimes when we pull ourselves up out of the fire we can see it once again. We must keep living our best lives and continue to put one foot in front of the other even when we stumble on this uneven path of life. There is good in people, and there is bad in people—no matter one's sexuality, what race, religion or career choice they make, and to be better we must refrain from judgment on those differences.

How, as a society, have we taught so much hate? Where and when did we lose the love? I'm not perfect by any means as a mom but one thing that I insist on instilling in my children is to be kind and understanding, care about people and always do one kind thing every day of your life.

Being kind is easy. If we can teach that one small thing to our children, then maybe we can find the love in the world again, or at least it's a start.

I saw this post from a gentleman in my community named Pedro Rosario, who allowed me to share his thoughts; it was empowering.

Funny little story I would like to share. I was driving the other day to a private session for my football kids and listened in on a conversation the kids were having. I had five kids in my car, two Dominican, one Puerto Rican, one black and one white. One of the Spanish kids had only been to the private coach once and could not remember who he was. The other four kids were trying to describe the coach to him. And here's how Joseph, Jonathan, Gary, Dylan and Brock described him.

"Well, he is not real tall but he's not short. He is big but not fat, more muscular. He has a beard but not long. He always wears a hat but different kinds. He sometimes coaches at the Saints Field but usually at this field." And it went on for a few more minutes.

Moral of this story: NOT ONCE did any of the kids say that the coach was black. You have to love the innocence of children and their minds. They don't see color or race unless taught that way. This is why I love coaching! To our kids, it's not the color of the skin but the color of the opposing jersey. We are all one race. The HUMAN RACE!

Amen to that! This world is one that we all share together—one that needs change, one that needs healing—and it is up to us to be that change. Be kind to each other, lend a hand where needed, smile just because you can. Change can only come when we stand united with each other and stop breeding hate. There is more love in this world than hate. I see it all the time. It's in a brand new baby's smile, it's in an old man's laughter and it is in everything else in between.

Like Mr. Rosario said, "It's not the color of your skin; it's the color of the jersey." It's your choice each morning which jersey you'll choose to wear.

So let's get on the same team and go to bat for peace and unity. The win is long overdue.

# Chapter 4
## *The Reason for My Season*

The month of February always makes me a bit sad, not because of the cold weather but because football season comes to an end. I absolutely love Football Sundays. It's not just about the game; it's about the people that fill my home. People have always asked me how I host Sunday after Sunday. I tell them, " I would have it no other way."

My house is filled not only with family and friends but with my children's friends, which is my favorite part. Football Sundays are simple and always come with a theme. Whether the moms are rolling out dough for homemade pizzas while cutting up toppings for the kids to choose from, cooking up sandwiches in the panini machine while taking requests like short order cooks or deep frying every traditional football food there is—including zeppoles, deep fried Oreos (I said it was traditional, not necessarily healthy), whatever the case may be—no one ever leaves hungry. We eat, we laugh, we watch football. Yet, most importantly, we spend our Sundays together.

Yes, we spoil them and serve them, but there are also lessons of compassion and kindness learned. For on Sundays during the holiday months, I put them to work.

No matter where you reside there are always families who are struggling. During the winter holidays we collect food for these families who simply need a hand up. Once the items are collected, my young football fans help me unload my car of the items so that we can sort them out and pack them up. Most years we have at least twenty-five families, some years more. It always humbles me to watch these friends carefully sort the items so that each family has one of everything to complete a nice holiday meal. Chatting among themselves, they talk about touchdowns and string beans, passes and stuffing. But while watching the game there are certainly no fumbles in the care they take to ensure their baskets are perfect. Watching football and watching out for fellow human beings simply go perfectly together.

I felt just a bit melancholy one particular year. It was Super Bowl Sunday, the last Sunday of the season. My son and his friends were now high school seniors, which meant it would likely be the last time this entire group would be gathered here together for Football Sunday. Next year it would be different because they would be off to college, doing their own thing and having their own parties while moving along their own roads of life. It made me wonder how time passed by so quickly and how these kids I've known since they were little had now become young adults. It made me sad because I knew how terribly I would miss these days. But I also knew how lucky I was to have been a part of them, and for that, this Sunday Football hostess felt so blessed.

After the Super Bowl was over, I put some desserts on the table as I told them how I would miss them next season and that the door of my home would always be open when they were home from school to catch a game. I began to clean up around them, thinking they were not really listening to what this emotional mom had just said. Having a little pity party for myself, I started to wonder if the days of Sunday Football meant as much to them as it had to me. The answer to that came in the next moment.

One of the boys stood up, handed me a gift bag and said, "This is from all of us." Inside of the bag was a gift certificate for dinner, which together they all chipped in to buy along with a card that read:

*Thank you for having us over every weekend and whenever we wanted. Thank you for constantly feeding us and never failing to make us full. We've enjoyed all the times at your house and appreciate all you do for us.*

*Thank you!*
*The Sunday Football Crew*
*P.S. Now have a meal on us.*

How did I do this Sunday after Sunday? How could I not?

Embrace the simple moments and the people that surround you.

Every season has a reason, and every reason has a season. I know my football season certainly did!

P.S. They still come back!!

# Chapter 5
## *Love Will Always Prevail in a Place Called Home*

"When my wife and I first came to this country in 2006 to make a better life for ourselves, we had nothing but the clothes on our back and a small amount of money in our pockets. We knew we would have to work hard to build our nest here in the United States. So strand by strand, piece by piece, that is what we did," tearfully explained a young dad who lived in an apartment complex where a devastating fire displaced fifty families.

"As my wife and I spoke last night while she was cradling our four-month-old son, we spoke of how even though we lost everything in the fire we were still lucky to be alive. I explained to her how we were like birds and, as we did when we first arrived in this country, we would again begin to rebuild our nest, strand by strand, piece by piece, dream by dream, and we would be all right."

Tragedy can happen to anyone at any moment. The twists and turns of life can come at us when we least expect it, knocking us to our knees and taking our breath away, leaving everything we knew in disarray. Nobody wants to find themselves in that place. But, unfortunately, sometimes we do, and that's when we find out who the unwavering people are in the world.

I never grow tired of writing about the humble and selfless people I have met throughout my life. Due to my job, I get to see the best of humanity in the worst of times. People reach out to strangers, mow a lawn for the wife of a veteran who is serving overseas, donate their hair, food, money or a toy for a child at Christmas and anything else a neighbor needs, whether they know them or not, just because that's what they do. It's an amazing thing to be a part of a community filled with so much kindness.

In those weeks following that terrible fire the acts of generosity and just plain human kindness never stopped. Not only did I witness it from adults but children as well. A young boy showed up where we were collecting donations for the families with a small envelope that contained thirty-one dollars and fifty cents. He told me it was money he had saved from his allowance. He slowly turned and started to walk away when I stopped him to ask him why he wanted to donate the money. He said, "One of my classmates lost everything in the fire so I thought maybe he could buy some new sneakers."

Another little girl came by with two dolls. She told me they were her favorite when she was little; she was only seven years old. She said she thought maybe a little girl who lost their dolls might like to have them to play with.

The rest of the world can say whatever negative things they'd like about kids these days, but I think there are so many more kids that shine with compassion and kindness than don't, and no one can tell me differently because I see it in them all the time. Where kindness leads, kindness follows.

Anyone can live in a town anywhere in the world. As we grow older, we think to ourselves we should relocate, find a place that has lower taxes and is less expensive, downsize our homes and live someplace less crowded. But if you buy a bigger house in another state where you know no one, who will you fill it with?

People have many reasons why they leave one community to go to another, but I think I will stay right where I am. I have built a solid foundation with roots that are strong. Should the winds of life blow in, I will be able to weather the storm because my foundation has been built on love and is enfolded by great family, friends and neighbors. It is not just a community where I call home. It is a village that links strong arms together to lift each other up. We can't always fix the pain that someone is going through, but sometimes a gentle embrace from the people that surround you can help bring you closer to the light and give you the strength we all need, now and again, to keep pushing forward.

Life. It truly does take a village!

# Chapter 6
## *The Most Wonderful Time of the Year*

What is it that makes the month of December so magical? What is it about this month that makes us a little kinder and more compassionate about our fellow man? Why is it that during this time we truly want to believe in Santa and that there really can be peace on earth?

It could be that while we're frantically shopping at the stores in the midst of our madness, we're also humming and singing along (though we may not realize it) to the songs that are being played on the radio there. Those same songs that we grew up singing, the ones we know every word to and the ones that make us feel young and childlike again. They can still make us smile, and some still bring tears to our eyes.

There is nothing like the face of a child who sits on Santa's lap and whispers in his ear what he wishes for the most. Wouldn't it be nice if we could all jump on Santa's lap again and whisper in his ear what we really wanted? Would you ask him for a new piece of jewelry? Would you ask him for a new car? Would you ask him for a laptop computer? Or just maybe would you use your one wish to whisper in his ear and ask him for peace on earth?

Each year when my children were little, during the holidays I set aside a day during the craziness of the season to bake cookies. I covered up the table and put out every cookie cutter I could find, along with sprinkles, frosting, candy (leftover Halloween candy works) and whatever else we can find, then we would crank up the Christmas songs and get to work. We made Santas with pink hair, purple Christmas trees, snowmen with three eyes and a few other things that were part of the first three things that have magically taken on a shape of their own. And if they weren't perfect, so be it! Those cookies had been made with love from little hands and excited hearts. They turned my boring old kitchen into a winter wonderland, sparkling with green and red sugarcane sprinkles, and on that day, while we were bakers, I only enjoyed the magic of the season and didn't worry so much about the mess. The kids and the kitchen, after all, could be cleaned later because the memories of those special Christmas moments would live on long after the sprinkles were gone.

Maybe that's why Christmastime is so magical; it's a chance to enjoy the moments that make up our lives. For me, the best gift I can still give my children is the gift of time. For each day fate allows us to share together is the greatest gift of all. The true meaning of the season is not about what we receive from others; it's what we give to others. It's not about what material gifts we have; after all, those are just possessions, things that easily get discarded through the years as we grow tired of them or they break. For in the end, it's not the trinkets you've collected through the years; it's the people you've collected, the lives you've touched and the friendships you've made. Those will always be more valuable, and personally, I'd trade every shiny trinket I was ever offered to keep those memories and the people I love instead.

Truth be told, if someone asked you what gifts you received last year, would you even remember? I doubt it.

But if you asked the little boy that stood quietly at a community center until Santa took him on his lap and gave him a shiny fire truck and a warm coat what he received for Christmas that year, he would tell you every detail. Not only would he remember those gifts, but chances are when he is old enough to understand more importantly, he will remember the kindness of strangers that gave him a reason to smile that holiday.

You don't need a lot of money to make a difference in someone's life during this time of year or any time of year. All you need is simply the gift of your heart.

Being a kind and compassionate adult is a great way to teach our children that caring about others is so important because it will help them grow into strong, compassionate and kind human beings, and the world needs that more than ever right now. Technology changes every day, and the world becomes more advanced, which is a wonderful gift for our future generations. But human kindness, that should never change. Generation after generation, compassion and love for our fellow man should always prevail; for if they do, goodness and hope are sure to follow.

Whatever holiday you celebrate, may you celebrate it through childlike eyes, and may your homes be filled with the laughter and love of those you hold most dear.

P.S. If you get a chance to sit on Santa's lap this year, don't forget what to wish for!

# Chapter 7
## *Beautiful Wrinkles*

I had just had lunch with two World War II veterans that I was interviewing. As I was leaving the diner, I ran into a woman I hadn't seen in quite some time. As we began to talk, she mentioned to me it was her birthday. When I smiled and wished her a happy birthday, she went on a rampage of how she hated birthdays and growing old was horrible. How her weight was creeping up on her, how her face was full of wrinkles, her body ached. She felt like her mind wasn't as sharp anymore, and things that she used to enjoy were no longer fun. I think she was in her forties.

As we went our separate ways I thought to myself, "Thank God I'm growing old."

It makes me crazy when people say growing old is horrible because what is the alternative? Life must go on, and if we want to continue to live, basically we must grow old; it's as simple as that.

Plenty of people in this world would do anything to have just one more birthday to celebrate with all those so-called issues that woman was worried about. I've met those people, and if she had met them also, she just may change her mind.

Ask the grieving mother who lost her daughter from an overdose of drugs about wrinkles. It would be hard to compare the two because when you die at seventeen, you don't have wrinkles yet. Or the woman who is battling cancer, fighting with every breath she has for just one more day to be with her family. Aches and pains? Hers cannot even come close in comparison with that of a woman whose aches and pains never subside. She may also reconsider that thought about the couple extra pounds she put on when she sees this woman's frail body that has now wasted away to skin and bones, the cancer making it impossible to "put on an extra couple pounds."

As for not having a sharp mind, I should have walked her inside to meet my veteran friends who I just left at the diner. Sad to think this forty-something woman thinks her mind isn't sharp and she can't remember things anymore. Maybe to enhance one's mind you must rid it of the negativity, then you can think more clearly.

Ed is ninety and Jack is eighty-six years of age, and their minds are sharp as tacks when the conversation revolves around their time in the military. Over lunch they speak of days gone by, of people that they have met, places they have seen and things they still need to do. The stories they tell are filled with such detail it's as if they lived them yesterday. And there is no stopping this dynamic duo. In the Golden Years of their lives they continue to advocate for veterans both old and young. Do not tell them they are old; their faces lined with beautiful wrinkles that reflect the wisdom and grace they have gained through life will certainly laugh right at you.

Lastly, too old for fun? Well, let me direct her attention to a local Senior Center called The Evergreen, otherwise known as "Ever Young."

This particular day when I stopped by the center it was filled with life, and everyone was dressed in red for their Valentine's Day party. There was singing and laughter, dancing and friendship, and for some reason I don't think at this party that any of my senior friends were worried about wrinkles. They are young at heart, living their best lives, and if they are worried about anything it's about too many tables stretching onto the dance floor, not allowing them enough room to swing around. Getting old is horrible? Don't tell them that because these seniors don't know what age is in this moment. What about another birthday? Bring it on; it will be just another reason for them to have a party.

My point is age is a matter of mind. You can be old at forty, or you can be young at ninety; the choice is yours. But keep in mind some people don't have that choice, and they would take every one of your imperfections to grow another year older. Beauty grows from inside you, and age can never reverse the beauty of one's soul with a wrinkle.

So celebrate your birthday, have a party, thank God for another year of life with friends and family. And if you need help blowing out the candles, just take your cake over to that Senior Center for the breath of life in that group will have no trouble helping you blow those candles out.

As they say, life is about the breaths we take, the time in-between the dashes and the grains of sand we are given in the hourglass of life.

So breath, live and use every piece of your sand!

# Chapter 8
## *The Young Peacemakers*

A few years back I stopped over to my son's high school to pick up a gift basket at the front office for a fundraising event. I was in a rush and wanted to run in and out, then get to my next stop. As I walked out of the office with my basket in tow, an alarm went off and a voice came over the speaker to say that the school was being locked down. I had heard about these drills and figured it didn't concern me. I would just slip back out the door I came in, but that wasn't the case.

A teacher in the hall instructed me to go with her. When I told her I needed to leave, she said I couldn't because once there is a lockdown no once can exit the building. So I quickly followed her to the teachers' lounge where other staff members that were on their lunch break had already gathered and were busily doing whatever they had to do in the event of an emergency. The door was locked, and I was instructed to follow the directions that were given to me. I was fascinated and horrified at the same time at what had become so routine to these teachers in preparation of keeping their students safe. As I sat there in silence, all I could think about was my son who was in the building, too. It made me wonder if he and the other students were afraid when they did these drills. Or had they become so accustomed to the world we live in that it just became a part of their normal school day, like we did growing up when there was a fire drill?

But when we were growing up, our drills were evacuation drills to help prepare us on how to get out of the building in an organized fashion in the event of a fire or bomb scare. In a lockdown drill students are told to hide and stay silent. These children know all too well the term school shooter.

It broke my heart to think that my son, born just before 9/11, knew this world too well; though still a beautiful world with much promise and hope, it made me sad that he knew the darkness of it as well. In that moment of clarity as I sat there against the wall, I wished with all my heart, just like any parent, I could shield his eyes from those images that come across our TV screens way too often. But sadly, I can't.

After the lockdown was over and we were let out of our room, I returned to the hall as the bell rang. Out poured students from every direction as they began to change classes. The silence was gone, and back to children they became. There were loud voices and laughter, smiles across their young innocent faces. Resilience, I thought to myself. What an amazing gift.

A few weeks after my lockdown encounter there was a mass school shooting in Parkland, Florida. I was unable to stop listening to the devastated voices of the high school students from this school and amazed by their courage and strength to raise up their voices as they became crusaders for change amid a tragedy that not even adults could comprehend. They had been vigilant, they had been angry. But, most importantly they had been powerful and persistent. They joined together and started a movement called Never Again to advocate for gun reform. Their voices were heard throughout the world.

They had had enough; we've all had enough. But as adults we have become so customary to these all too familiar scenes that we just hold our breath, gasp, and then walk away and go about our lives. Change, sad to say, never comes.

But maybe this new generation of young adults will be the ones that will bring about that change. There is a spark in them, a willingness to truly want to redesign the world. I commend them for seeking to make this world a safer and more peaceful place for us all to live.

So let them talk, let them try, let them shine as bright as they can as they raise their voices to make a difference in our world.

We all have opinions and different beliefs, and that's OK. We should. But at the end of the day I believe in my heart that whatever our beliefs are, we all want the same thing: a peaceful world for our children, for their children and every generation of children that follows.

So here's to the young peacemakers who strive to make a difference today, for it will be their time to inherit the earth tomorrow!

# Chapter 9
## *Celebrate*
## *the Uncelebrated Moments*

My summer has been filled with great celebrations. My youngest son graduated from college this year, along with his many friends, so there have been so many graduations that we were able to celebrate. There have also been retirement parties, wedding showers and lots of weddings that we were able to celebrate. The common denominator of all these wonderful celebrations of life is that *"we were able to celebrate."*

It seems so long ago yet like yesterday when those days of celebration were left uncelebrated. We were unable to share the beautiful moments in our lives with those we love. The days that should have been the most cherished and happiest were put on the shelf for another day because a pandemic swept over us and stole away the thing we love the most: each other.

I was recently reminded about the days we lost while going through a journal I had kept, along with pictures I had taken, during that time. I suppose the writer in me knew it would be important to write those thoughts down for I had a feeling that years later someone would ask what it was like. Or maybe the journal was just for me to remind myself what the meaning of life was and, of course, through my book remind you. So here's your reminder.

In a moment's time the world changed, but as it did, so did we. Businesses closed, sports were gone and parks usually bustling with children fell silent. To get food and supplies we needed to wear masks and gloves. Casual conversations in a grocery store were no more; we just wanted to get in and out. Parents became teachers while trying to juggle working from home. College students who should have been enjoying the whole "college experience" now tried to find a quiet place in a full house to do homework. Visiting our parents, something we didn't do enough of before, was something we couldn't do at all. And the good-byes we couldn't say, along with the hands we couldn't hold because of the disease we could not understand, left so many families feeling helpless and heartbroken. And it still does today. We lost a lot through those days; none of us were untouched. The hours and days that had passed that we spent in quarantine, some of us with family, some of us alone, were filled with life lessons for all of us, young and old collectively.

*Here are some of the lessons that I learned during my days of quarantine:*

• That we need human touch more than any material item in the world.

• That no matter how strong our arms are, if we can't hold each other, we become weak.

• That arms are meant to stretch out to hug and cheeks are meant to be kissed.

• That hands feel better held than fist bumped.

• That birthdays, graduations, weddings and everything that brings us joy were meant to be celebrated together, not alone.

• That children need to swing on swings and footballs need to be tossed in the air to someone else.

• That I loved having my children just to myself for a while.

• That neighbors should be talked to instead of waved at.

• That saying good-bye to someone you love through a glass window is the hardest thing you will ever have to do, and that losing someone you love was not meant to go unnoticed; their life should be celebrated.

• That people are kinder than we assume and more important to us than we know.

• That life is about family, true friends and even strangers that come into our lives, if even only for a moment.

• That tomorrow is not promised to any of us and each breath we take is a gift.

• That we are like a tree: We have strong branches, weak branches, broken branches and branches that are yet to bloom into something even more beautiful.

Yet he biggest lesson I learned is that we truly just need each other. We need to hug, we need to laugh, we need to be together and we need to care about each other because even in the darkest of times, when the world is filled with fear and uncertainty, we just need the love of each other to bring us back to the light.

So I will never again complain that my days are too filled with events that take every weekend and take joy in the fact that *we are able to celebrate.* Celebrate your life, live every day the best you can and just be kind to each other. The gift of life is the greatest gift we have. Put it on a shelf or open it every day; it's your choice. But it's best opened every day!

# Chapter 10
## *Just Breathe*

Life is a precious gift that is too often taken for granted when we are running from one place to the next. We forget to make the time because it feels we don't have enough of it—for our family, friends and loved ones. We turn down an invitation to lunch because we have errands to run. We don't spend enough time with our parents. We tell our children that we're too busy right now to read them a story, throw a ball with them or simply listen to how their day was. We are tired, and we have so much yet to do so the day goes by. When we finally put our feet up at night, can we tell ourselves that any of those tasks were more important than calling your mom, missing lunch with an old friend or reading your child's favorite book to them before they had gone to bed? I don't think so.

Take a moment to just breathe in every day. Inhale all your worries slowly, then one by one exhale them out until your soul becomes just a touch lighter. Let your breaths remind you of the beauty you have inside, what is important to you. Let your newfound energy guide you on how to be a better friend, a better sibling, a better parent and, most importantly, the best version of yourself.

Just breathe.

# Chapter 11
## *Myself on a Shelf*

Each year from my office window as I watched kindergarten parents walk with their children back to school after the summer comes to an end, with hands tightly clutched in their own, I wondered who was more afraid, the parents or the children.

We feel so many emotions as parents when change comes into our children's lives, even good and positive changes. There is pride as we watch our children make a new step in their lives and fear of letting go of their hand as they walk away on their own. It seems like yesterday I was dropping my son off at preschool. He had been quite ill as a baby with breathing issues, and my fear of letting someone else care for him took my own breath away.

I stood quietly in the hallway after he went into the classroom for what seemed to be hours as he had been crying so hard that I knew there was a chance he would have difficulty breathing. After about fifteen minutes (it wasn't really hours), his teacher came out, gently took my hand and assured me I could leave; he had stopped crying, and they would take good care of him. As I turned to walk out of the school another mother asked me if he was my first child to go to preschool. I realized she had been standing in the same hallway with me, probably with the same tears in her eyes. I smiled at her and said, "No, he's my third child. You'd think I'd be getting better at this." She understood just what I meant, one mother to another. You don't get better at it.

Not even when you send them off to college. I quietly cried the entire way there and the entire way home after dropping my daughter off at college, my first child to go away. I would have stayed and cried in her dorm room, too, but she begged me to go as she handed me my coat and said, "Jeez, Mom, I'll be back soon. Relax."

The school years have all now concluded for my children. This year, the first in what seems like a lifetime, I have no one to buy supplies for, make a lunch for or drive back to school. And as that comes with a touch of sadness, I know it's just the turn of the page. I am certainly proud of the paths my children have chosen for themselves. I am excited to see where their next beautiful steps will lead as, once again, I let them go into the next chapter of their lives.

When you become a parent a big part of who you are is put away on a shelf as a new part of who you are to become begins to emerge. When your children are small, most days you can't take a breath without them needing something. Your days are built around playdates and baseball schedules, carpools and soccer parties, runny noses and tears. But they are also filled with laughter and a love deeper than you have ever known. Then one day, without you even noticing, they start to become their own little person, each day needing you just a little less than the day before and spreading their wings just a touch to feel the wind beneath them. As much as we want to hold onto them forever, the day will come when we must gently let them go.

I suppose it's time I revisit with that person I left on that shelf so many years ago, for it's not only children that need to find their next steps in the journey of life. Once they are grown, their parents do, too.

Time moves swiftly. One day you're watching your child ride away for the first time on their bike, then you watch them ride away into their futures with weddings, babies and all new beautiful blessings that, by the grace of God, will once again bring you playdates, soccer parties, runny noses and a continued love deeper than you have ever known. Life changes but it sure can be beautiful. No matter where their roads lead them if it's traveled in love, it will always lead them back home.

# Chapter 12
## *Simple Treasures*

It wasn't an earth-shattering story, one that I'm sure many didn't even take the time to read, but for some reason it caught my eye.

I read an article in the newspaper about the life and death of wine legend Ernest Gallo. I never really thought much about him before except perhaps while purchasing a bottle of wine. I remember that day being tired of reading about the craziness of the world, so for a moment I decided instead to read about this man who died at the age of ninety-seven years, after making wine his whole life. The article went on to say he was a son of an immigrant father who came to America from Italy and that he and his brother grew up working in their father's vineyard. Years later Ernest and his brother, Julio, founded the E. & J. Gallo Winery, once known as the world's largest wine making empire. The article highlighted his success by the size of his empire.

I don't know how all the days of his life were lived; I'm sure there were struggles and heartbreak along the way, as in anyone's life. The thing that did impress me the most about his life, though, was the end as I read these words:

*Mr. Ernest Gallo, Wine Legend, passed away peacefully this afternoon surrounded by his family at the age of 97. Mr. Gallo was married to the love of his life for 62 years until she passed away just a few years back. He had two sons, five grandchildren and three great-grandchildren. He and his brother started their company 70 years ago and continued to work side by side throughout their lives as they stayed close and built their families together. The families of both Ernest and Julio now will continue the work.*

When you think you don't have all you should, when you just want a little more of what everyone else has, look around. Remind yourself that even if your empire is a simple home with walls covered in hand-painted dragons and princesses and your greatest treasures are the artists that painted them, you have the greatest empire of all. No amount of money can buy you more.

Sometimes in order to find your own meaning of happiness you need to look past the things you don't have in your life to get a clear vision of the blessings that you do.

Enjoy the simple treasures; they are everywhere you look.

# Chapter 13
## *Pieces of the Puzzle of Life*

It was a crazy Friday morning; my phone was ringing off the hook, and I still needed to finish my April issue of the paper that afternoon. This month, in honor of autism awareness, I was making a collage out of the faces of children in the township who had autism. I carefully placed their beautiful little faces in colorful frames on my front page. Suddenly, I realized I was late to take a picture over at the local middle school so I grabbed my camera and flew out the door, stressing about what I was going to write to go along with those pictures. Like magic, when I arrived at the school everything about my day changed, or maybe you can just say it came together like a puzzle.

The school, which has a population with special needs, had called me the week prior to see if I could come take a picture of the students who were going to assemble outside in the school parking lot to participate in an event called "Blowing Bubbles For Autism."

The school prides itself with a program called "Friday's Friends." This is a remarkable program that allows students to work with other students within the school with special needs. Their mission is to help teach compassion and understanding for someone who may act or look a little differently than themselves, while all along building new friendships.

In order to get the perfect picture, I needed the help of the local fire department, which was on scene when I arrived. I climbed into the bucket of the truck as they lifted me high in the air. After the students were done blowing their bubbles, they then would come together to make the shape of a heart. I was told that the students would each get a piece of colored paper so that the heart, once assembled, would look like a colorful puzzle, a symbol of autism.

And that it did.

As students moved around and held their different colors up in the air, the puzzle slowly began to form together into a beautiful heart filled with all the colors of the rainbow. Within the heart were faculty, students, secretaries, janitors and the special education students that made the heart sparkle even brighter. Together, each one of them stood as a symbol of unity, tolerance and under-standing for the world of autism. What a beautiful sight to see.

If you're not a parent of a child with autism, which I'm not, you can never truly understand the full meaning of their world. I have met parents through the years with autistic children, and I am amazed by their powerful strength and love. Their unfaltering determination to make sure their child receives the tools they need to help them get through life and to be treated like every other child is a never-ending fight for them.

After getting down from the fire truck I walked back through the crowd of children and watched as the students interacted with the special needs students. They were hugging each other, high-fiving and laughing, just as children are supposed to do. Here in this moment they were all just children, all pieces of different puzzles, yet all colorful pieces just the same.

If you think about it, we are all different pieces of the puzzle of life. No one person in this world makes up the same shape in the puzzle. We are all molded differently. Yet, somehow when we are put next to each other, our puzzle becomes complete. For how boring a puzzle would be if the pieces were all the same, no color, no different shapes, no beauty, no adventure; it would be like staring into a dark circle, which would make for a very boring predictable world.

So embrace all the unique pieces. The ones that add color, the ones that add truth and the ones that give us beauty to shine. Let our differences be a way to bring us together and teach us compassion so that we can find a global unity of peace in this world that we all share. For the puzzle of life would never be as complete or as beautiful without each of them.

# Chapter 14
## *Fear Doesn't Stand a Chance*

**If nothing ever changed, there'd be no butterflies.**
### *~Author Unknown*

When you're stuck in a spot in your life and don't know which way to move, sit quietly for a moment and breath in the air. The answers will find you.

It was 2013, the beginning of a new year. I felt stuck in a spot and overwhelmed. I had a decision in my life I had to make at the time that seemed so difficult. It was the fear in me, the uncertainly of a new step, that was holding me back and weighing me down. Fear can be paralyzing when you face it head-on but in a few moments I would come to realize that fear doesn't stand a chance against courage.

I was hosting a Super Bowl party and was in the kitchen by myself as I was preparing food for my guests. My house was loud and bustling. I could hear the basketball bouncing on the living room floor next to my kitchen, the ball that I told my son to make sure he put away before all the kids came over. Somehow he must have forgotten that warning, and it seemed as if there was a full court basketball game going on in the next room instead. I'm a pretty relaxed mom so I figured we'd talk about it later; today was today, and they were having fun.

I brought some of the food downstairs where the adults were, then circled back into my kitchen to bring the rest to the "basketball team" in the other room. As I did, I realized the room had fallen silent. The once bustling living room, which moments before had held laughter and mayhem, now held those same young friends staring at the TV. As I placed the snacks down on the table, I was drawn into the same vision that held their eyes captive.

There on the football field, before the start of the game, stood twenty-six young children. They were clothed in tan pants and white shirts that were adorned by a tiny green ribbon as they performed *"America the Beautiful."* Their voices were angelic, their composure strong, yet in their innocent faces there was a sadness that could not be dismissed.

For these were not just any children; they had seen more than any child or adult for that matter should ever have to see. They were the children of Newtown, Connecticut, where just seven weeks prior they lost twenty classmates and six adults from their school in a massacre that rocked the entire nation.

With tears in our eyes we watched as these young students gave the performance of their lives in front of millions of strangers. When the song concluded, we talked about the shooting, now etched once again in all of our minds. As their conversations moved back to the game and away from what they had just witnessed, life went on. Children are resilient; they have the ability to push through things that we as adults can't get out of our heads. Sometimes I wonder if that's a blessing or a curse.

As I walked out of that room, the only thought I had was how courageous those twenty-six children were, how courageous their parents were and how courageous people can be when they stand together to hold each other up to get through something that no one can comprehend. But they did just that. They stood up to the world as they represented their small community to prove that they were stronger than hate and better than evil, and that good would always prevail when encircled with love.

Those twenty-six young voices, in a world filled with billions of voices, were heard that day, and they mattered.

Fear can be a powerful force when making changes in your life. It can stop you in your tracks, it can change your fate and it can prevent you from ever knowing what could have been. It's not easy to find the courage within yourself when you're unsure, and it's not easy to take a step forward in a direction you've never been. But life is about taking chances and about change—if we never emerge from our cocoon, the world will never see the beauty of our wings.

On any given day life can change in a moment. So live, love and be the best person you can be. Never let fear stand in the way for where your heart leads you to go. For it is through positive change that we continue to move forward, continue to be better and bring peace to the world.

# Chapter 15
## *The Red Ribbon*

Everyone has something they are afraid of; some of those fears can be justified while others are just small little insecurities that make us nervous. I can spend hours writing just about anything, but when put in front of an audience I tend to get nervous, and the words that I knew so perfectly before can come out very differently. Many of my friends feel the same way. I have one girlfriend that gets nervous just walking through a crowded room because she feels like people are watching her.

I suppose that's the reason we all have some type of fear, such as speaking, singing, presenting a project, standing up at a board meeting or simply walking through a crowded room. It's the fear of what people think of you. Sounds silly, but many of us have that fear because, let's face it, deep inside we all want to be liked and accepted by the people around us.

I was busy working on an event called Support the Troops Rally. The event was first started after the 9/11 attacks when troops were being deployed to Afghanistan. The rally was a way in which the community could support those within it that were serving overseas. This particular year would be the first time I would oversee coordinating the event, and I wanted it to go perfectly because of the importance of it to so many families.

The morning of the rally I sat at my desk, nervously finalizing everything for that evening. I had to leave for a bit before the event to attend a ribbon cutting at a new senior center facility that was being named after a local young marine named Cpl. Kevin Reinhard, who had tragically lost his life in Afghanistan that past year. There was a beautiful ceremony, and heartfelt words were spoken by many people including Kevin's mom that led up to the ribbon cutting of the new facility.

As I stood next to Kevin's parents as they got ready to cut the ribbon, I thought to myself just how hard this had to be for them. As the ribbon fell to the ground I reached down and grabbed a piece, handed it to his mom and told her she should keep it. Then for some reason I reached back down and picked up a piece of that same ribbon and put it in my purse.

As I jumped into my car to get back to my office the phone rang. It was a gentleman named Charlie Kenny. Charlie was the person who brought the program to life years prior and had been doing it from its inception until I was given the reins to continue. Charlie convinced me, as the rally came closer, not to be nervous. He would be there to guide me through this first year. But after picking up the phone, Charlie, who is also a fireman, explained to me that there was a bad fire and the likelihood of him making it to the rally on time, if at all, was not good. He assured me I'd be fine and that I could do it on my own. But suddenly, my nervousness turned into sheer panic.

When I got back to my office, I threw my purse on the desk and frantically went over the items I needed to bring with me while trying to convince myself halfheartedly that I would get through this just fine. I made my kids a quick dinner, then ran back down the stairs to grab my notes before heading to the rally. That's when I saw the red ribbon laying on my desk; it must have fallen from my purse. For some reason, I don't know why, I grabbed the ribbon and attached it to the clipboard that held my notes.

As I sat at a traffic light on the way to the rally, I felt this sense of calmness come over me for the first time in weeks as I glanced over at the ribbon on my seat. Suddenly, it made me realize that this rally wasn't about me; it was about veterans like Kevin and all those brave men and women who have and would continue to serve our country.

I kept that ribbon with me on my clipboard throughout the program, never putting it down. It was as if that tiny ribbon caught a corner of my eye each time I looked down, and it gave me newfound courage. As I spoke to the crowd that had gathered in support of their loved ones, I felt incredibly honored and proud to be standing there before them. I was no longer afraid to be the voice for the veterans. In fact, I felt as if Cpl. Kevin Reinhard was standing there right beside me with his hand on that same piece of ribbon to help solidify what the true meaning of the evening was about.

I suppose we could all use a small piece of red ribbon to remind us just what in life is truly important and to help keep us grounded when small fears creep in that seem larger than life. Sometimes it just takes a gentle reminder to tell us that we can battle through the fear if we trust in the strength we have within ourselves.

# Chapter 16
## *Somewhere Behind Their Eyes*

Finally, after years of looking at a box in my office of old videos that could no longer be used in a VCR (dating myself), I decided it was time to convert them to digital. I thought it would be a fun surprise to take them on vacation and do a movie night with my family. For years my family vacationed together with my parents, two sisters, brother and a whole lot of little ones.

Sadly, life changes, and as time moved along so did our vacations. Someone was heading back to college, one was involved in travel sports and some had other vacation destinations. But regardless, those years together that we did have were amazing—and all caught on camera.

I took my digital memories to my sister's beach house in Bethany, Delaware. My entire family wasn't there but a bunch of the cousins who are now adults were. We buttered the popcorn, poured some cocktails and laughed for hours.

Most of the videos were taken during the times spent on those family vacations in Myrtle

Beach and the Outer Banks. They were filled with carefree days on the beach. One of the constants was my dad running around with his grandchildren, acting like a wild man jumping in and out of the ocean. My dad loved the water and made a point to teach all his grandkids how to swim in the ocean safely as well as what to do if they were ever in trouble. Of course, he taught them to body surf as well. He would put the kids on the boards and push them in over a big wave as my sisters and I yelled at him, hoping he wouldn't drown them. But he never took his eyes off them, not even for a moment. Those vacations were filled with so many wonderful memories, and we were blessed to have them.

As much as we laughed at those videos, it also made us feel sad that my dad, their grandpa, is longer with us. When he got sick many years before he was no longer that same man, the one that acted silly and carefree. Instead, he slowly became angry and forgetful as the cruel disease of dementia stepped in to take over the person he once was. Sometimes he remembered those days, other days he didn't.

When someone is sick for such a long time, we tend to forget who that person used to be before they grew old. Through the years when our dad was sick our thoughts were mostly of his well-being, and the memories of days gone by were put on hold. The new memories we made with him now were much different from the old ones. As hard as we tried to remember the man he used to be, it was difficult; as the years passed, we lost him a little more each day.

My girlfriend's parents came here from India when she was five years old and her brother was seven. Not knowing anyone here except one friend, this man bravely left the rest of his family and everything he knew in his life behind in search of a better one for his children. It was not an easy journey, and I'm certain there were times when he missed his family and life in India. But he powered through and worked very hard to achieve success in America. He ended up being a well-respected engineer in New York City and retired just prior to his eightieth birthday.

He is now eighty-seven years old and no longer knows who he is. This once vibrant, intelligent man is but a shell of the person he used to be. Not because he chose this or deserved this, it's the hand that life dealt him. His conversations are now repetitive and seemly unimportant. He talks about food and struggles to remember those days of his life that brought him so much joy.

Somewhere spinning around in the minds of those who lose them are beautiful memories just desperately trying to reach the surface, yet they are drowning.

When we look at someone older, we don't always see who they were; we see them for who they are now. But there was a time, and we should all remember, that those beautiful souls who have now grown older were once lawyers, craftsman, carpenters, firemen, nurses, teachers and the best mom, dad, grandpa or grandma in someone's universe.

After he died it took me about a year for the good memories of my dad to resurface. I was finally able to remember the happy, fun, life-of-the-party guy he had been, and I know that is exactly how he would have wanted to be remembered.

So next time you see someone who has lived their gift of life, don't dismiss who still lives behind their eyes. Somewhere they are still there!

# Chapter 17
## *Through the Eyes of a Policeman*

"I'll never forget that powder. It was like grey talcum powder. It was everywhere, so deep that you couldn't even tell where the street curb was; it was hard to breathe," recalls Lt. Skolsky.

Lt. Glenn Skolsky, a Woodbridge, NJ, police officer, was sitting at his desk when he heard the news that an aircraft had crashed into the first tower of the World Trade Center. The day was September 11, 2001.

"I went to the room at headquarters where there was one cable TV to find out what was happening as other officers gathered to do the same. I watched in disbelief as a second plane slammed into the second tower. I felt sick and knew at that moment that the magnitude of what had just happened was soon to unfold."

Shortly after, the prosecutor's office sent out an urgent request for volunteers to assemble a mutual aid force to go into New York City. Nine officers from his department, including Skolsky, were told to "go home and pack your bags for three to five days." The officers went home and did just that. They returned to headquarters where a bus awaited to take them to a central location at the nearby Fire Academy where police from all over the county mustered together for assignments.

Lt. Skolsky stood among his fellow officers under the bluest of skies on a picture-perfect day, preparing himself to walk into a place of extreme terror and horror—not sure what to expect but knowing something wasn't right and this was going to be bad but also hoping that his twenty years as a police officer would be enough to prepare him for what he was about to encounter. It wasn't.

The nine Woodbridge police officers were sent to Yankee Stadium on Staten Island where they had set up a collection point for the dead. From there they were ferried over to Battery Park where they assembled under the Brooklyn Bridge with officers from all over.

"It was the eeriest feeling, like a scary movie as police officers walked toward Fulton Fish Market in complete silence. There were no cars, there were no trucks, there was no noise, just silence and powder in the air," Lt. Skolsky explained as his strong face recalled the memory too well.

A high-ranking NYC Police Chief gave assignments to the different squads, and the nine police officers from Woodbridge were sent to secure the borders at Church Street, just a couple of blocks from where the Twin Towers once stood. Their assignment was to allow no one to pass the area except for emergency personnel.

As they stood watch, they took turns going back and forth to the pile of rubble that was once the World Trade Center to see what they could do to help, or just to stand there among their fellow brothers as they all watched in horror of what the terrorists had done to America. The thought was more than anyone could bear. But that was their job, no matter how horrific it was. They were New York, New Jersey and Port Authority police officers who were there to help the people in that building. So without thought or fear they did what they were trained to do.

Aside from taking turns going to the rubble, the nine men never split up, Lt. Skolsky explained. "I came here with nine guys, and I'm going home with nine guys." Luckily, the Woodbridge police officers did just that. A combined total of 403 firemen, police officers, Port Authority police, EMTs and paramedics did not go home.

There are many things from that day that stand out in Lt. Skolsky's mind. He remembers standing next to part of the engine from the airplane that hit the building. He remembers the sight of the overturned police cars that were shattered and tossed like matchbox cars from the impact when the towers collapsed, and again the powder that now piled upon them. He also remembers standing in front of St. Patrick's Cathedral staring into a once vibrant and bustling city that had been silenced and blown apart around him. Not a man of strong religious beliefs, he found himself staring at the church, the only thing around him that was still intact, not a window broken or a door damaged. The only thing that gave evidence of the day's horror was the paper and clothes that now covered the trees that surrounded the building.

The nine officers stayed in the city for two days. Then, for a few months, the New Jersey State Police Brotherhood Association sent two golf carts and a trailer daily, along with police volunteers, to bring food, drinks and supplies to those who continued in the search and rescue effort. Several officers also went to Staten Island over the course of time to help sift through the debris for remains.

"I'm angry at the terrorists for what they did to so many innocent people," Lt. Skolsky explained as he recalled the events of that day as if it were yesterday. "So many people just went to work to do their jobs that day, just like they had in the days prior to the attack. For no reason, innocent lives were ripped away from the people that loved them. Innocent rescue workers who went into a burning building to simply save the life of another human being and lost their own in a heroic effort. It just makes no sense."

Lt. Skolsky explained to me that he doesn't want to appear angry about it. But he is, just like everyone is. "If this event has taught me anything it's that I'm more aware of my surroundings, and I have more patience for people that do security checks in airports. I'll wait in line, I don't have a problem with that. They are doing a good job if I have to wait for them to search someone in front of me." He also went on to explain that "it has also strengthened the respect I already had for my brother officers and firemen, who every day continue to do what they do and do it to help those that they swear to 'Honor and Protect.'"

Since September 11, 2001, Lt. Skolsky had not gone back to Ground Zero until his daughter Samantha, who lives in Arizona, came to visit and wanted him to take her there. At the time he hadn't realized that almost ten years had already passed by, and he had never taken the trip back. He wasn't sure he could do it, wasn't sure if he wanted to do it. But his daughter wanted to go, and he wanted to be the one to go with her. They took the train in, and it wasn't until he got onto the PATH that it hit him. Once he got off the PATH he told his daughter he just needed to stand there for a moment, just needed to gather his thoughts before he went on. So Lt. Skolsky pulled himself together and walked back toward the place that forever had changed him. As he and his daughter walked toward Ground Zero he found himself standing at the exact place where he stood almost ten years before: St. Patrick's Cathedral.

Lt. Skolsky and his daughter went inside the church that afternoon and looked at the memorabilia that was now displayed in honor of the victims of

9/11. The church still looked as it had on that dark day of September except now the trees that embraced it were green and full of life, a valid reminder that life had gone on around it. Among the evil and the pain it stood strong and stayed intact, just as the police, firemen, rescue workers and all of America did that dark day of September 2001.

# Chapter 18
## *A Twinkle in a Wrinkle*

A few weeks ago I was with a friend of mine whom I hadn't seen in a couple of months. While we were catching up about our kids, she was telling me that her daughter and her friends, all in their early twenties, go to Botox parties. It seems that's the new craze. Apparently, they serve food and drinks, like we used to do, but not with candles and pizza stones. Instead, the item for sale is Botox to fix their imperfections.

Being curious, I googled what exactly a Botox party was, and this is what I found: "A Botox party is a social event where people get together, often at someone's home, to get Botox injections. Depending on how the party is organized, the injections 'might' be given by a licensed physician.'"

Might be? That's scary in itself!

I won't quote the whole article, but the last line said, "You can't buy happiness, but you can buy Botox, and that's kind of the same thing."

WHAT? The same thing?? Ok, maybe I'm showing my age, but I find it hard to understand why beautiful young girls in their twenties would be worrying about wrinkles, getting Botox and looking younger while they are presently swimming in the real fountain of youth. Truthfully, I always thought Botox was for rich, aging actors in Hollywood— again showing my age.

Fast-forward two weeks, I was at another friend's house, and two women there were talking about the same thing except their conversation was more about work they already had done and what they would like to get done next. Maybe I'm missing something, but through my eyes people are beautiful in their own right. I would never judge a stranger, much less a friend, for a wrinkle on their face or because they put on an extra pound, and I would hope they wouldn't judge me either. For in reality, if we did judge each other that harshly, how would we ever keep our friends? Has society put so much pressure on us to be so perfect that we are in constant pursuit to capture it? And when and if you do, is it enough?

I'm not saying it's not important to take care of ourselves, but it's just as important to take care of our mental health. Doing something positive to better ourselves, taking time to smell the roses and, most importantly, just to appreciate the people who we love and to know they are healthy and happy, that will give you a beautiful glow that you will never find in a bottle.

I remember when I was a little girl, one of my favorite people in the world was my grandmother. It's funny thinking back now; she always looked like a grandmother even though she was in her early fifties. But I never saw a wrinkle on her face. I'm sure they were there but I just never noticed them because her face was so soft and cheerful, and I never thought about her waistline as her arms wrapped around me like a soft blanket. To me she was just simply beautiful.

So when we search for perfection because we don't feel like we are beautiful enough or fit enough or rich enough or any of those things that we believe will make us happier with our lives, take a moment to think about all those people that are battling something in their lives, whether emotionally or physically, that would give up perfection and all the riches in the world for the gift of good health, happiness, love and, yes, a good old-fashioned wrinkle.

Growing old is a gift, denied to many. So use your gift wisely.

# Chapter 19
## *Temporarily Disconnected*

It's a strange thing to be disconnected from the world. For most of us while packing up for vacation, one of the most important things we check is to make sure we have our cell phone and charger. We could have everything packed in the car and forget one of our kids; but by God that phone and charger are going to be packed and the extra charger plugged in the car just in case our phone dies on the way to our destination. To step away from the world without our phones is unthinkable, but when we do a whole new world opens up.

A few years ago, my family, all nineteen of us, embarked onto a cruise ship that was set to sail for the beautiful island of Bermuda. We learned as we boarded the ship, that there would be no wi-fi for the two days at sea as well as the two-day return trip home. I felt like I was in that commercial where the kids would not get on the plane because they would not be able to use their phones. But off we sailed into the sunset, totally disconnected from the world.

It took a while for us, adults included, not to look at our phones. We could no longer post everything we saw and tell the world every detail of where we were and what we were doing. We all still had our phones with us with the small hope that somehow Wi-Fi would magically appear, but it did not. It is amazing the conversations you can have at the dinner table with your children and adults when no one has their phone in their hands.

I was thinking about that cruise the other day when the news of the world was draining my soul and I just wanted to turn it off for a while. I truly believe that one of the healthiest things you can do for yourself is take a break from the negativity that is so easily spread on social media and just catch your breath so that you can refocus on what is important in your life. It makes me crazy when I'm sitting with people, in the middle of a conversation I thought we were having together, they start talking about something that they are looking at on Facebook and the subject changes to: "Did you hear about...?" Or they start smiling at their phones and giving a "thumbs-up" to someone else's day while missing out on their own.

Some people are so intertwined in the lives of others "Look At Me" status that the simple beautiful things around them go unnoticed and quality conversations go unheard. Nothing against social media but being unconnected to the world for a week while I was on that trip with no Facebook, Instagram, texts or emails was not the end of the world; in fact, it was a blessing. To be honest, after the first day on the cruise ship the kids did not even think about their phones as they were too busy living their lives and having fun rather than wasting those summer days glued to a phone watching the lives of everyone else while missing out on their own.

Disconnecting yourself from the world is one if the healthiest things you can do for yourself. It gives you a chance to take a breath, refocus, enjoy the simplicity of life and just live.

So put your phone down and for a while take a break from the world. Instead, go for a walk, read a book, float in the pool, have a long conversation with someone you love and take a moment to appreciate the blessings that surround you every day. They are all right there—just waiting for you to reconnect to life again.

# Chapter 20
## *The Foundation of a Mother*

No matter how old we are, we still need our moms. As children they nurture us, protect us, make us feel safe and, most importantly, they love us unconditionally. Being a mother is one of the hardest yet most rewarding jobs you can ever be blessed with.

A mother always worries about every aspect of her child's life. She worries that they are warm and cared for, nurtured and loved. She worries when they cry as babies and worries more when they cry as teenagers. She worries that when they are school age they will make friends and others will treat them kindly. She worries when her child isn't invited to the party that the other kids are invited to, when they don't make the team they already had the pom poms for or the bat that they were going to hit the home run with. They worry when they apply to the college of their dreams or meet their first love. They worry when they get in a car and drive away for the first time alone. They worry the same if they have a belly ache or a heartache.

And just when they think they can stop worrying, their babies have babies, and the worrying starts all over.

But during the days of COVID-19 the worry was different, brought on by a world they no longer understood nor could control. Worrying about getting invited to a birthday party no longer crossed their minds as now their worry was how to teach their child, or for many moms their children, how to do virtual learning while juggling their own jobs. They worried about teaching their child how to wear a mask so that they would be safe, yet at the same time trying not to instill a fear in them of the world outside their door. They learned to teach math and science, English and gym—all while trying to keep their families healthy and mentally stable. They had to answer to their teenagers why they couldn't see their friends or kick a soccer ball around the field, then had to deal with their child's anger and frustration when they explained why those things they loved had to be put on hold—all while trying to deal with their own emotions. They had to wear a brave face and convince their children that things would get better. In order to do that they built snowmen, they baked together, they did puzzles and played more games than they did as a child themselves. And most did it with gentle grace, courage and strength that they never knew they had.

And then in their quiet moments when their children were finally asleep, they would lie awake at night worrying about the health of their own parents, silently praying that the virus would not claim them as it had done to so many others. Some spent sleepless nights crying because, sadly, it already had.

But in the morning the mom would get up, put on her brave face and do it all over again because she had to keep her family moving through her fears, through her tears and through her anger so that it would strengthen her faith to assure the ones she loved that there would be a brighter tomorrow. Because in her heart she knew there had to be.

Like the tall grass that waves in the summer winds, no matter how hard the storm blows in, the roots that grow in the foundation of a mother's love will not be unrooted.

# Chapter 21
## *You Can Only Write One Book*

I'm an optimistic person, always trying to see the bottle—oops, I mean the cup—half filled. It's just a better way to travel through life. My life is happy because it's full, and much of my happiness comes because I am blessed not only with a wonderful family but with cherished friends.

It's funny how you go through friends in your life. They say friends come in and out of your life like characters in a book; some stay until the book ends while others are there for only a few pages. But nevertheless, they are just as important because without them the book wouldn't be complete, and the story wouldn't move forward. Some friends will leave the story of your life, and that's OK; there was a reason for them in that chapter. Yet, others will remain, filling the pages with memories that you could never write the book of your life without.

My friends are fun and full of life; they know how to have a good time. And the best part of it is our kids like to hang out with us (that is, until we start singing after a couple of glasses of wine and they move to the next room). I mostly love that my friends' children are best friends with my children. In fact, that's who introduced most of us, and after all these years we may not be family by blood but we are certainly family by heart.

Through the years we have shared happiness and heartache, accomplishments and failures, and together we have shared some of the greatest celebrations of our lives. It has not always been easy. There have been disagreements and division, sometimes anger and hurt, but at the end of the day we have always had each other's backs. Through the wisdom of my years I have found when you surround yourself with good people, you become better.

The world is not easy but journeying through it with people that love you makes it a whole lot more manageable. When you feel alone and life hands you more that you can shoulder, those moments define the meaning of a true friend. They are the ones who step in, simply take your hand and let you break down while they encircle you with their strength and love. When you grow tired they bring coffee and conversation. When you grow too weak to fight, they fight for you. When you are afraid they reaffirm that you are stronger than you think and braver than you know. When the pen of life falls from your hand, they pick it up and continue to write the story for you.

Cherish those friendships because, like beautiful flowers, if you don't nourish them and add water to their roots, over time they will fade away. Make time for your friends, love them, respect them and, most importantly, enjoy them. Laugh a *lot*, make dinner for them on the china that's been collecting dust, pour wine in that Waterford wine glass and let it make you sing and dance and definitely embarrass those kids that love you. Fill the pages of your life with happy moments, family and *true* friends.

You can only write one book. So make it a bestseller.

# And Finally...
## *Through my Daughter's Eyes*
### By Kayla Meehan

There are two different types of reality. One is the physical world, and the other is the one that lives within us. Everyone sees the world differently based on our imprints in the seeds that create our fundamental base. The human race is like a forest; even though some trees may look the same, there are still slight differences that make them unique from each other.

But unlike trees that move and change with the physical world, humans can choose which way they want to view the sun. We can go through life running toward our next task, accomplishing one goal after the other. But the best lesson I have learned through this journey is the importance of slowing down. We move so fast that we sometimes forget about the light that comes through our windows in the morning and the smell of coffee as it brews. Take a moment to breathe, find wonder in the changing of the seasons and know there is always a gift to be found within our happiest days and our greatest challenges.

# Acknowledgments

Finding the courage to do something you have always dreamed of is not something you do alone. The unknown is both terrifying and exciting in the same breath.

When I took my laptop and ran away for two nights by myself to a tiny cabin on the lake, truly in the middle of nowhere, I wasn't sure where to start with this book. As I settled in to write, I found the only directions I needed when I turned my computer on: "Good luck with your book writing. I am so proud of you, Mom. I love you. Kay."

I hit the little icon on my screen named "Debbie's book" and began to bring it to life.

I have published a small-town newspaper for over twenty-two years, along with its column called Thoughts From The Editor where I simply write about the stories of life. Some of the columns are written about difficult days. Others are just life lessons that I learned growing up, or stories about an everyday person or event. For the most part the stories in this book form a collection about the lives of people in a small town. Though they take place here within my community, they could take place in any small town across America.

Rereading many columns that I had written through the years helped me think back through so many different moments in history, be it in the country or in the lives of those I know or had known. First, I thank those who contributed to the stories that allowed me to write them.

Next, I thank all my family that have encouraged this journey from the start. My children have been the biggest inspirations of my life, and my wish for them is that they continue to always see the good in the world, even when days are challenging. It is through their eyes that I have found the meaning of my life, which has guided me to find the best in the world for them. I want them always to see the beauty, the butterflies and a world that is filled with hope for their futures.

Thank you to all my amazing friends (and neighbor Bill) who fill the pages of my life and add so much color to all my chapters. Kelly, you just know my thanks for you!

Thank you to Karen Hodges Miller of Open Door Publications. When I first spoke to her two years ago and told her what I wanted to do, she said, "You already have a book written. What are you waiting for?" She has guided this new author through the unknown and gently pushed me through each door I needed to walk through to get here.

And I would be remiss if I didn't thank you, the Colonia community and Woodbridge Township. Your stories are a cultivation of the stories that grace these pages. I have laughed with you, cried with you, drawn strength and knowledge from you, and together we make up a village of people that embrace each other through not only the good days but the hard ones as well. I am truly blessed to have raised my family here with all of you!

My wish to my readers is that within these pages you find inspiration and hope and that it helps to adjust your lens to allow you to see the beauty that surrounds us each and every day in this world we all share together. When we open our eyes and search for the things that encourage us rather than deflate us, it brings so much more beauty to our lives. So always look for things that shine!

# About the Author

Debbie Meehan has been the owner and author of a hometown newspaper in Woodbridge Township, New Jersey, for over twenty-two years. *The Corner* newspaper reflects the positive and personal stories of those who reside in her community, along with all the good news that takes place from within it. This is the first book she has published.

Debbie resides in Colonia, NJ, with her family.

www.ingramcontent.com/pod-product-compliance
Lightning Source LLC
Chambersburg PA
CBHW060338130626
46553CB00003B/1045